Parakram, a recent IT Graduate, embodies a stereotypical notion of what an Indian is supposed to be. Even his middle name is Raj! Coming from a Bengali cultural background, possessing the art of writing which seems to be a natural calling…debuting on the public front with his first book comprising of poems, the intent behind the collection is to establish a certain sense of derivative uniqueness in a pool of stereotypical topics. Prosaic by nature, Parakram believes this book proudly juxtaposes exactly that.

Parakram Raj Dev

CROMULENT CAMEO

AUSTIN MACAULEY PUBLISHERS™

LONDON • CAMBRIDGE • NEW YORK • SHARJAH

A CIP catalogue record for this title is available from the British Library.

ISBN 9781398472679 (Paperback)
ISBN 9781398472686 (ePub e-book)

www.austinmacauley.com

First Published 2024
Austin Macauley Publishers Ltd®
1 Canada Square
Canary Wharf
London
E14 5AA

Austin Macauley Publishers rightfully qualifies to be garnered with all my regard and gratefulness, without whose pragmatic support this book would have been yet another dust crusted manuscript at the bottom-most drawer of my office desk.

Table of Contents

Monster

Looked for the monster under my bed,
Who as an adult I no longer dread,
There was no sign of him, underneath and within,
I just wanted to ask him to be my friend.

I just wanted to make sure if he was well fed,
"I am lonely and lost," reluctantly he said,
It sounded familiar and then I put together
That the voices were coming from inside my head.

– PRD12

Uselessness

I almost mastered the art, the art of uselessness,
But failed at the end, because of my carelessness,
I was young and a fool, used hesitance as a tool,
And now all I feel is numbness and senselessness.

Along came youthfulness,
With all its might and ruthlessness,
It didn't care and gave me a stern glare,
As if to say I still had it in me—usefulness.

It pulled me up, for I laid in my misguided mess,
I stood and sat on the chair,
As if I was the next chosen heir,
And in my kingdom entered blissfulness.

I no longer felt my senselessness,
Gone were the days of my carelessness,
I felt happy and full of life, set free from all the strife,
As I mustered all I had learnt and set ablaze the art, the art of utter uselessness.

– PRD12

I Remember

Yes, I remember, as in the mayhem,
When everyone was in search for the diadem,
The towers were searched, discipline besmirched,
Overlooked by the fools, the room of requirement.
They broke out in a run and then began the fun,
What stood in front of them was now irrelevant.
They saved Malfoy's gang, stabbed the crown with the fang,
And now the Dark Lord lost his temperament.
All but the snake was now left in the wake,
For the Dark Lord's death to be permanent.
Or so they thought, that victory is what they got,
Sadly, they were unaware of the determinant.
Determinant of the endgame,
When Harry was to die with his fame,
He walked towards the woods, with memories of his childhood
Voldemort hit him with the curse and he was dead was the claim.
A chat with Dumbledore and he realized it wasn't over—the war,
On he went on his ascent,
As he was more fearless than ever before.
Nagini was killed, prophecy fulfilled,
And Voldemort had nothing more in store.
They fought till the end, to their heart's content,
But Voldemort was bound to the floor.
His wand had betrayed, cause its master, Harry had been made,
And there lay the weakling, the idiots adored.
It was an epic tale to tell; the tyranny was brought to a quell,
The scar had not pained Harry for 19 years. All was well.

– PRD12

Better/Latter

12

Claim to be different than better,
Only then will the world be the latter.

Claim to be different than better,
Only then will everyone be less indifferent but the latter.

Claim to be different than better,
Only then will everything around you seem to be the latter.

Claim to be different than better,
Only then will you progress to be the latter.

Claim to be different than better,
Only then will the world be the latter.

– PRD12

!Drown

I'd rather not dare,
For it will not compare,
To the strives that has been made, the knowledge they cascade,
And eventually it becomes too much to bear.

For just like our lives, our minds are finite,
We always seek the fight to find the light,
For we would like to think it to be infinite.

Uneasy lies the head that wears the crown,
A crown that might take us down,
For it ain't no child's play, if we truly desire to know its way,
In an ocean of ideas, we need to swim and not drown.

– PRD12

I Wonder

I wonder what kind of life they live,
Life inside a mirror,
I wonder if it's a peaceful world
Or rather that of horror.

I wonder if they yearn for morality as well,
Or if they have a whole new story to tell.
I wonder if emotionally they are on the same path,
Or if they are just ravages of time thriving in a bloodbath.

I wonder if the grass is greener on the other side,
If they knew something with which they could guide
Us to better ourselves as humans and provide
For we have no more time to bide.

I wonder if they are full of life or lazy,
Level-headed people or just crazy,
I wonder if they are full of energy like the thunder,
I wonder if they wonder what I wonder.

– PRD12

Twice the Man

I could swear I was there,
There as in the top of the stair.
Well, then let me think if I did actually blink,
And that would indubitably explain my despair.

I was way up to the top,
When obstacles came out with a mop,
It saw my privileged state, and without a debate,
It pushed me down a massive drop.

I was yet again where I began,
With no one around from my clan,
I felt despised and then I realized,
That I was now twice the man.

– PRD12

Nothing to Worry

There was no one else I could turn to,
There was no one left from my crew.
I did not know how to handle the pain,
Since the beast inside me had been slain.

I was already frail and now I was broken too,
I had absolutely no idea what else I could do.
I tried to gather my strength and fight back,
But my ever-so-strong determination had begun to crack.

The volcano inside me was about to explode,
But I was not yet ready to go down that road.
Finally, it erupted and everything went blurry,
I was deep in my sleep and there was nothing to worry.

– PRD12

How are They so Sure

How are they so sure
Of something that's so obscure,
They all know what to do and say
And everything else is to their dismay.

How are they so sure
Of what to and what not to procure,
They all know the perfect way to live,
What to be happy about and what to grieve.

How are they so sure,
Of what we can or cannot endure,
They all know the nuances of being civilized
That cannot and will never be compromised.

How are they so sure,
That they are willing to immure,
Anyone who questions them
And if need be, even create mayhem.

How are they so sure,
That all they want to do is allure,
That they want everyone to know,
Of their wisdom, which really is their ego.

How are they so sure,
Or are they just insecure,
For being incompetent to comprehend reality is scary.
For obduracy makes us our own adversary.

– PRD12

No Longer Digress

I was worried that they might not come back
Embarrassed with everything that they clearly lack,
But they showed a brave heart, and jokes apart,
This time they really yearned to get back on track.

How can they improve, I wonder,
Pausing to make sure that I did not make a blunder,
But they seemed sincere and without any fear,
This time it felt like they wouldn't fall asunder.

With a healthy intake
For everyone else's sake,
They worked to reform and weathered the storm,
And after a really long time, they felt awake.

After eons, I felt like I had access,
That I was no longer under acute stress.
I hope this is the dawn, for each of my neuron,
As I aim to no longer digress.

– PRD12

Insatiably Curious

Am I really here
Or should I just not care?
Should I just go about and be carefree
Or should I just go all in and bend the knee?

'Cause after actively trying to find the answer,
I finally feel like an unpaid freelancer.
'Cause I just cannot make out a head or a tail,
And it just feels like I'm unequivocally gonna fail.

Am I really here,
Or should I not dare?
To question the people in charge
Discussing their asserted opinions at large.

'Cause more often than not,
I find myself contradicting my thought.
So naturally, an adamant daft makes me furious,
Void of inquisitiveness makes me insatiably curious.

– PRD12

Meant to Be

I was very generously told
That you have a heart of gold.
So I came here and I am utmost sincere
When I say that my will will never be sold.

My will will never be sold,
Even if I am left out in the cold,
You can punch me down, make me look like a clown,
Yet, I will still remain bold.

For it took me a long time to get here,
For the utter ignorance to finally disappear,
I am finally in the game and I sincerely aim,
To no longer be a dolt sightseer.

I stand before the world to see,
This time I won't kneel before thee,
Even if it gets really bad, I would still be glad,
That I finally became the man I was meant to be.

– PRD12

It Is What It Is

There was treasure to be found,
That was supposedly buried underground.
I kept looking for it before I had to forfeit,
When I realized I was failure-bound.

Am I falling or am I not?
Is it just the thrill that I sought?
I kept on asking as I was basking
Under the warmth that the sunshine brought.

I finally felt weary,
After all the work that was dreary,
I kept it within, underneath my fuzzy skin,
That nothing ever again could get me all cheery.

All I wanted was a sight of bliss,
Apparently, it was a swing and a miss,
As a critter who's inept, it's just tough to accept,
That at the end of the day, it is what it is.

– PRD12

The Nose Knows

I was once stuck
Between a metaphor and simile.
Furious, I was confused if
I felt like a beast or was just beastly.

It felt as if my whole life was a lie,
And ultimately I had to lie
Down and it was almost a week,
But I still, to my dismay, felt weak.

A terrible nightmare and my sleep breaks,
I finally realize that I need to hit the brakes,
Before it's too late, as time gone by,
Is undeniably something we can never buy.

Worried, as occasionally, my Spidey senses go off,
Trust issues and insecurity are what it's actually made of,
I agree that its pros can tend be a bit prose,
However, if something's fishy, as always, the nose knows.

– PRD12

Ignorance is Bliss

Ignorance is bliss
As then there is nothing to miss,
You can go about with your day,
Thinking in black and white and nothing in grey.

No time to ponder
And no new place to wander
Into finally doubting if you are capable,
If your character is truly pliable.

No what-ifs and does-it-matter,
Your thoughts could only but scatter.
Weaker than a hydrogen bond,
If ever in that place, you couldn't possibly respond.

A tedious schedule and living in the moment,
Being indifferent must be quite pleasant,
They get happiness in abundance, I imagine,
While I am still on the road searchin', just drivin'.
– PRD12

Couldn't Care Less

I couldn't care less,
For it's not worth the stress,
To try and appease everyone,
Descend to their level to have fun.

As at the end, it won't matter,
Even if your dreams shatter.
The sun will still rise and go down,
Like clockwork and won't even frown.

'Cause nobody really cares
If the quandary isn't theirs.
As then there is no need to ponder upon.
No reason to intrude but move on.

Well, with this awakening, it has become very clear,
Things can be very different than the way they appear,
And worth is not to be understood, for if you should,
Go down that route, it would amount to no good.
– PRD12

I Ponder and Wonder

25

I ponder and wonder.
Then remember to surrender,
To the core idea of war,
That had bored me never before.
But this time, it was sublime,
For I'm in my prime
To decide to go with the flow
And not to throw away what I owe,
Not to him, her or thee
But to yours truly.

For I dare to care,
And share rather despair,
To look out for me and see
The degree to which I had to flee
To not be attacked but rather distract
Myself from the fact that I am in the final act.

I let out a heavy sigh, as the time passed by,
Finally able to comply with the truth and not ask why.
For there was nothing to defend or anything to mend,
As the destined end was about to impend.
Finally to assess, to express and not impress,
I confess, my stress was but a well-played game of chess.

– PRD12

As Dark as It Can Ever Get

I am everything I hate and more.
More enraging than ever before.
Utterly disorientated and a complete mess.
I couldn't care less even if I was careless.

In this chaos, I took a walk down the memory lane,
When everything and everyone seemed so sane,
What I would give to get them back,
Absolutely nothing, as empathy is what I now lack.

History is about learning from the mistakes of the past,
And not for the gleeful days and achievements to broadcast.
Nostalgia makes the present look bad and impels us to sigh woefully.
Entraps us to go down the rabbit hole of endless melancholy.

A tiring day that amounts to nothing,
A lifetime to figure out everything,
With the hope to at least understand something,
Only to receive agony in return, as that's all it can bring.

I fathom nothing more can be done,
I reckon only a confusing web will be spun.
If we continue down this lane,
It would only lead us to inconceivable pain.

I have a morbid sense of humour,
Is the ongoing rumour.
True, for if we have ever met,
I'm sure you would bet,
That I'm as dark as it can ever get.

– PRD12

Why is It so Dark in Here?

Why is it so dark in here?
Do you not fear,
Of what you might stumble upon?
Like the truth about being nothing but a pawn.

Well, the truth is all relative, I guess,
But the lack of social construct would be a mess.
And hence, we must all abide
By the norm and set aside our pride.

As the truth is whatever the most powerful says
And you need to decide whether to rebel or digress.
Well, there is of course the third option,
Where with patience, you utilize your pawn's formation.

With collateral damage, create a smoke screen,
With their guards down, you can take the king out clean.
Congratulations, you are now in charge
Of the truth and everyone else, looking at the mirage.

But always be on high alert.
Make sure this transition remains covert.
You need to make them believe they came up with it,
That everything is in the right place and tightly knit.

As the revelation of what you did won't go well.
They will now no longer digress but rebel.
Or maybe, just maybe, they will go with the third option,
And the cycle goes on, as you fall by virtue of your own creation.

– PRD12

Home Again

A recent abrupt revelation took me aback.
Filled in the void with something I used to lack.
I was not sure if I was seeing it right,
It stuck out like a firefly in a cold winter night.

With spellbinding features it transcended.
The sceptic in me wanted to ensure if I was being misled.
As its arrival seemed too good to be true,
Inconceivable to the point that I had no idea what to do.

But I had to gather back my senses.
March forward and accept the consequences.
The notion, which I was sure I could never discern,
That now pain was the only norm, the only concern.

I had to calm myself down and process.
To ensure I act from a place of solace.
The inner joy in me couldn't be seen.
No one could know how restless I'd been.

Things looked familiar with a hint of the unknown.
It dawned upon me that it too had immensely grown.
A soft reminiscent sigh, I inexorably felt sheltered then.
Unfathomable as it might seem, I was finally home again.

– PRD12

Gremlin

A way for us all to forget,
To relinquish the outstanding debt,
That anyone has ever owed to you,
Is to treasure their joy instead of feeling blue.

You might continue to meddle.
Full steam ahead rather than backpedal,
On the train of thought that makes you ask why,
Why they don't recognize your grind but deny.

As a constant desire of validation,
Is what inherently needs elation,
To apparently move above and beyond,
Face the grimmest of hurdles and still respond.

To be able to overcome and let go.
To not stay stubbornly confined but grow.
To summon sacrifice with a sardonic grin,
And all this to eventually impair the gremlin within.

– PRD12

Silence

The pleasant and blissful harmony,
To be able to perceive it is the key.
To not lose your mind altogether,
But be able to sway with it rather.

Mistaken thou shall be
To think it brings harm to thee.
It is nothing but a clean slate,
For you to calmly create.

With a bit of patience and a clear mind,
You can sense the euphony intertwined.
Capitalizing on the scope it brought,
You can contrive your own Camelot.

I get why people often miss the mark,
Especially when it is so cold and dark.
At times, it can surely be quite antsy and intense,
But nothing compares to the beauty of pure silence.

– PRD12

Mystique

What's there to smile,
Before you have completed the mile.
You still have a long way to walk
After you've separated from the flock.

No reason to look back,
To stare at the trailing pack.
They will catch up if they want to.
Maybe even get ahead and overtake you.

What's there to smile,
When you are losing meanwhile.
To realize how and when to make the right call
To be able to stand up, head held high and not fall.

The external noise that might come,
From everyone opposing you and then some.
To be able to hold your ground then,
Will be the final test of your true acumen.

What's there to not smile,
To have the choice to go out in style,
To look back and cherish the past,
Even the nightmares that last long.

Well, some argue we do have freewill,
And others couldn't be further down the hill.
It might very well be a craftily thought out applique.
Regardless, happiness is but mystique.

– PRD12

An Eye for an Aye

If only never-ending bliss I could keep,
I would feel much more content when I go to sleep.
I would be as far as I could be from the torment.
But alas! I could only but circumvent.

To be polite and well mannered, they say.
But the fine line is now blurred and grey.
To leave a mark and set aside the distraught,
Only to end up as a woefully fallen despot.

To fulfil that one uncompromising lifelong dream,
Owing a lot of debt seems to be the common theme.
To have the vehemence for the obstacles to overcome,
Eventually realizing: you win some; you lose some.

It seems the price is too high to pay,
For the odds to sway the other way.
At the end of the day, even if I could fly,
I couldn't deny that it was an eye for an aye.

– PRD12

Preserve Sorrow

It's a burden to preserve sorrow,
If it's worth it, I don't know.
It seems like a secret not to be uncovered,
And now I am paying the expenses incurred.

What is more easy?
To face it head-on or duck?
To actively seek out the crazy,
Or to not push my luck?

Seems like a tough choice to make,
To be like a diamond and not break.
For if there was ever an easy way to have a really good day,
I would probably never be awake.

– PRD12

Nostalgia

There once lived a little feeling,
Which then was a lot less appealing.
She was, oh, so kind to advise and make me realise,
Not everything is quite always revealing.

In a nurtured environment she grew,
Constant agony was not something she knew.
Went as far as to dare, to live a life without despair,
But her gloomy days were long overdue.

And so one fateful day, destiny arrived,
And only one explanation could be derived.
To bring stability was the goal and allow her to control
How she intended the inevitable to be contrived.

After tripping in the dark over and over again,
She was in time getting familiar with the pain.
Imminently after a while, as she was in her last mile,
She finally learnt when and when not to viably refrain.

At long last, she was no longer afraid to roll the dice.
For even something so bleak as someone's demise,
That she never coveted and would have otherwise regretted,
Was now within her realms to romanticize.

We were always really good friends but I never knew,
As the number of times we met lately were but very few.
Yet, the last time she was sent turned out to be very pertinent.
For she had now grown up to be nostalgia, if you hadn't a clue.

– PRD12

Last Winter

After it rained last night,
The morning sun didn't seem as bright.
A distinct dusky dawn was upon us,
The chilly winds materialized thus.

The unremarkable silvery ambiance
That was predominantly missed once,
Conjured up the frosty essence and more,
Accompanied by the emanating petrichor.

For a juncture that can be callously austere,
Ironically, it was still the rapturous time of the year.
But an unsettling thought disrupted the ecstasy.
An instinctive fervour put a halt on the intended destiny.

It was a sudden realization of what it meant.
The tangible relevance of the current event.
The end of a pertinent familiar phase,
And nearing the exit of this grand serpentine maze.

The opulence in the inherent comfort zone,
Was now to be capitulated and not condoned.
For now was the moment for wisdom to set ablaze,
As promptly approached my last winter days.

– PRD12

A to Z

All Battles Come Down,
Even Fabulously Groomed Hometown.
Intensely Justifying Knowing Lots,
Moronic Naive Opaque Pots,
Quivering Restlessly Shivering Tamely
Under Valiant Wanderlust Xenia
Yielding Zinnia.

– PRD12

A Simple One

When I was a little boy,
Playing used to bring me joy.
Now that I am a grown man,
Affording playtime I no longer can.

Aiming to utilize my time,
While I'm still in my prime,
Instead of spending a dime,
I tried to create schemes that rhyme.

I was inherently hesitant to begin with,
As I was definitely no wordsmith.
"What could possibly go wrong?"
Was the thought that finally got me to move along.

Hence, I began to finally write.
Sadly, they were too cryptic for people's appetite.
But now the idea is to satisfy and stun.
So, here I am, writing a simple one.

– PRD12

Bees

A rustling within the tress,
Underneath lived the bees.
An intricately designed hive,
Their whole lives, for which they strive.

The discipline manifested within,
The persistent will to be perfect lies therein.
Strictly a coherent functional colony,
Protecting the queen, their ideal destiny.

Apiaries we might acquire,
For little troopers at work to admire.
We surely could learn a lot,
From the enriching honey-filled pots.

But within all the sweetened glee,
Lies a surreal truth which is the key.
Squired with the embellishing refined honey,
The inevitable stinging bite shall be felt by thee.

– PRD12

If Not

39

The water that I breathe
The air that I drink
If not careful,
I might eventually sink.

The disreputable truth
The honest lie,
If not mindful,
Only peril would abide by.

A dandy personality,
Committed to a tedious chore,
If not cheerful,
Nugatory would pounce and more.

A lamentable heaven
A dignified hell,
If not grateful,
Purgatory seems swell.

– PRD12

H.B.M.G.

I was once aspiring for harmony,
Fed up of all the ongoing agony.
Illusive of my craft, unbearably daft,
Like Hitler with his beloved Germany.

Unwisely stuck with nostalgia,
I was gradually approaching dystopia.
Fearful of the effulge, agitated to indulge,
Like Bobby Fischer and his morbid paranoia

Reality and fantasy were no longer linking,
It was as if I was invariably sinking.
Down the river, I couldn't stop to quiver,
Like Mozart and his perpetual drinking.

My morality was on the fence,
Menacingly lacking common sense.
Deluding the world to be mine, pure and divine,
Like God and his cosmic omnipotence.

– PRD12

Birthday Cake

41

Ten years on,
Pacification gone.
Living in pretence,
A hollow existence.

Optimism of a happier tomorrow,
Now, nihilism and sorrow.
Dreams of a Camelot,
Now, abdicated wrought.

A character to be reckoned with,
At the epitome for a wordsmith.
A jocose figure void of strife,
Attitude larger than life.

Gone are the days,
As our spirits would raise.
Past the misty dawn,
We firmly trotted on.

Through the acute heartache,
Something had to take,
A man out of me to make.
For my own growth's sake.
My last birthday cake.

– PRD12

In the Winter Cold

In the winter cold,
Through heaven's spree,
Turbulence without,
Somnolent content for thee.

A life without fear,
Free of darkness within,
A tumultuous wind,
Shall make thou curiously keen.

Enigma of the unknown,
Carefree emotional opulence.
Above all plebians,
The red-pill effect awakens.

A bridge towards the agony,
Stairs away from chagrin,
A mere stare behind,
Stands the one with a formidable chin.

A heartbreak intolerable
The loss irreplaceable.
The tragedy of it all,
The promise of being amicable.

The denunciation of the norm,
The irony of the uniqueness,
Lies within us all,
The fortuitous culpability endless.

– PRD12

Extinct

43

It is easy for it won't be spent,
Neither given away nor reprimand.
A clock through the dagger hastens,
Before the cloak of light be wakens.
A nasty splint holds what is there not.
A rusty sprint tumbles only to fall short.
The pages of destiny lie in yellow like ever before.
The cages of certainty holds the white crows forever more.
A landslide chagrin in slumberous peace.
Demands for transgressed locks and its keys.
Depravity might very well pay the impending bills.
It might even prove to be a fettered stress kill.
But the further the apple falleth from the tree
The more intense is the rotting spree.

If I was a tree, I would be a
Banyan; strong, sturdy and distinct.
If I was an animal, I would be a
velociraptor; smart, feathered and extinct.

The Final Blow

Growing appalled by the tendencies of the blue ribbon,
Inspired only by the innate motive to syphon
The funds that waters the epitaph to prominence.
The hives around the stone exuberating pertinence.

A land over, embodied by those who know not to live.
A land under, forbid prose for lives that are ruminative.
A sea full of heat that fragments joy effervescently,
A decree to pass by that dictates impunity from saliently.

The stones to unnerve the cakes of ironic pastry;
Seemingly served with arduous tea in hubris cutlery.
With the string quartet of doom basely despondent,
D minor played for the cannon or requiem, the need advents.

An ominous glass lent, characteristically concave.
A fiendish brass bent to accommodate the ego's slaves.
A daring bridge whose ropes haven't felt the chill of the snow,
The gold base beneath the foreign silver, takes the final blow.

Flagrant Sounds

Complain but not throat slittingly.
Resist fate but not willingly.
A Rembrandt cascades, though it fades,
Past the cracks of chalky slates, forgivingly.

A clock whose hand points at you,
while couple others rendezvous;
Past the roads of slender dreams,
Aghast the doors of tender screams.

Notice a line, that follows you through,
The outline of your shadow that it withdrew.
A mind put to it, eventually flew,
To your silhouette's nest, whose venue it knew.

And down comes the hammer slinging, Odin son's pride.
Out with the thunder clinging, mischievous stride.
Mother dearest's ride knows no bounds,
From the wheel's squeak, voice the masses, flagrant sounds.

Don't wake me up!

Don't wake me up, for I am still dreaming.
Dreaming that I am awake and everything's gone to rot.
Is it really true or am I just another heavy-headed despot??
The kind that adds value by multiplying to the void.
The kind that spews out Nietzsche's words and quotes Freud.
Am I dealing with the hypnosis of self?
Or is my brain really in a jar on some shelf?
Is the cavalry of fatalism still busy scheming?
Or is the scheme too delicate for rhythm or rhyme?
For I see the inner workings of a giant clock
and the thing it intends to hide, is but lost time.

Cromulent Cameo

Dance, as I shall never can.
Fly, as I shall never would.
Dream, before the windmills fan.
Scream before the turbines could.

Tomorrow is a debt time owes, never to be paid.
The graves of the present turmoil will eventually be laid.
The incessant dreariness longed to break off but couldn't;
The decedent virtue craves for diamonds to be but wouldn't.

Swinging out the window, subtle lets the wind blow.
Clinging on to the aglow, battle sets the shend slow.
The words of post reckoning, shall judge his sole peer.
The cards of haste awakening shall lie in tried pure.

The roads of fervent flights, call upon to borrow;
The tired stars of the ever-dwindling scenario.
Magnum opus awaits, Carpe Diem alike,
Insolently poised, auguring my cromulent cameo.

Made in the USA
Monee, IL
07 July 2026

56552676R00026